NATHAN LEVY THINKING AND WRITING ACTIVITIES FOR THE BRAIN

BOOK 2

BY NATHAN LEVY AND AMY BURKE

Nathan Levy

PUBLISHED BY N.L. ASSOCIATES, INC.

A Note From The Authors

The activities in this book correspond with the notable quotations above each set of activities. Please use the designated space below the activities as guidance and note that these activities are NOT meant to be limited to the designated space. This book is meant to open minds and encourage creative thinking. We hope you will enjoy the activities in this book.

NL & AB

Copyright © 2004 N.L. Associates, Inc. Publishers
All Rights Reserved

All rights reserved. No part of this book may be reproduced in any manner whatever, including information storage or retrieval, in whole or in part (except for brief quotations in critical articles or reviews), without permission from the publisher. For information, write to N.L. Associates, Inc., P.O. Box 1199, Hightstown, NJ 08520, or call (732) 656 - 7822.

Printed in the United States of America

About the Authors

Nathan Levy is an internationally known educator, public speaker, and author. He is now a full-time consultant on topics relating to education and communications. He draws on his previous experiences as a school principal, corporation president, business owner, teacher, and workshop leader to enhance the critical and creative thinking of adults and children in a wide variety of workshops. In his published works (most notably the <u>Stories with Holes</u>, <u>Whose Clues?</u>, <u>Nathan Levy's 100 Intriguing Questions</u>, and <u>Not Just Schoolwork</u> series), Mr. Levy has provided thousands of educators, parents, and children the opportunity to explore activities which promote vivid writing and clear thinking. Nathan's ability to encourage a broadening of the creative and critical thinking process in schools and businesses has kept him in high demand as a workshop leader on a national level. He can be reached at:

N.L. Associates, Inc.
P.O. Box 1199
Hightstown, NJ 08520
(732) 656 - 7822

Via e-mail at: **Nlevy103@comcast.net**
Or via his website at: **www.storieswithholes.com**

Amy Burke has taught in both public and private schools in different parts of the country. She is happiest teaching middle school. Amy has facilitated workshops for teachers and parents, and has developed and taught writing and communication courses in university-based programs for gifted students. Ms. Burke is currently living in North Carolina with her husband Mike, and dog, Oreo, where she is teaching 7th grade Humanities in a Paideia-based school. Amy also serves as both the Paideia Coordinator for her school and the Teacher/Student Portfolio Coordinator. She has two children, a daughter, Rachel, and a son, Seth. Ms. Burke has presented at Paideia and other conferences, in addition to being the author of almost twenty books. She can be contacted through N.L. Associates, Inc. to arrange for her to speak at schools and conferences.

How Many?

"Man was endowed with two ears and one tongue, that he may listen more than speak."

—Zeno of Citium

How Many?

In a group, discuss the following:

Reasons to listen.

Reasons to speak.

Stay absolutely quiet for three minutes and listen to the sounds around you. At the end of three minutes, write about what you heard.

_____
_____
_____
_____
_____
_____
_____

Have a class meeting to analyze and discuss the listening behaviors of the class. Discuss the following:

1) When does the class listen best? Not at all? With difficulty?

2) Who are some of the best listeners?

3) What makes someone a good listener?

4) Why is it important to listen in school?

How Many?

Choose one or more of the following:

1) Write about whether it is harder for you to talk to a group OR to listen.

_____
_____
_____
_____
_____

2) Write about how you feel when people don't listen to you.

_____
_____
_____
_____
_____

3) Write about something you wish you could hear.

_____
_____
_____
_____
_____

How Many?

List the names of 10 people you speak with often. Beside each name:

Place an "L" if the person listens more than speaks.
Place an "S" if the person speaks more than listens.
Place an "IL" if you listen to this person more than you speak.
Place an "IS" if you speak to this person more than you listen.

1) _____
2) _____
3) _____
4) _____
5) _____
6) _____
7) _____
8) _____
9) _____
10) _____

Write one sentence that tells about YOU as a communicator.

_____
_____

What?

"The answer is there is no answer."

—The Answer Person!

What?

Write a poem in which you ask at least five questions you would like to have answered.

_____
_____
_____
_____
_____
_____
_____
_____
_____
_____

Make a list of at least five questions for which there are no answers.

1) _____

2) _____

3) _____

4) _____

5) _____

What?

Write about the meaning of at least one of these sayings:

1) "Just when I thought I knew all of the answers, they changed all of the questions!"

_____
_____
_____
_____
_____

2) "The answer is that the answer changes."

_____
_____
_____
_____
_____

3) "Life is uncertain, eat dessert first!"

_____
_____
_____
_____
_____

What?

Class discussion:
Einstein said that imagination is more important than knowledge. Do you agree?

Reason this out with a partner:
If a tree falls in a forest and no one hears it, does it make a sound?

Choose one or more of the following:

1) Write how you feel about living with uncertainty.

_____
_____
_____
_____
_____

2) Write about one thing you wish you knew for sure.

_____
_____
_____
_____
_____

Tomorrow And Tomorrow And Tomorrow

"One of these days is none of these days."

—English Proverb

Tomorrow And Tomorrow And Tomorrow

Discuss the meaning of these quotes:

"Procrastination is the thief of time."

"The best place to find a helping hand is at the end of your arm."

Do something you've been putting off RIGHT NOW!

Write one sentence telling how you feel now that it is done!
_____
_____

Write an essay: (Choose one or more.)

1) Something you should have said and didn't.
_____
_____
_____
_____

2) Something you should have done and didn't.
_____
_____
_____

Tomorrow And Tomorrow And Tomorrow

Make a list of three things you put off doing.

Answer the question "WHY?" after each one.

_____
_____
_____
_____
_____

Choose one or more of the following:

1) One of these days I'm going to...

_____
_____
_____
_____
_____

2) Something I almost always avoid doing...

_____
_____
_____
_____
_____

Tomorrow And Tomorrow And Tomorrow

Write and illustrate the first page of a self-help book called:

"Ways to NOT Put Off Doing _____"

_____
_____
_____
_____
_____
_____
_____
_____
_____

Assess your style of getting things done by answering:

1) Is it easier for me to start things OR finish things?
_____

2) Do I work better alone OR with someone?
_____

3) Do I wait until the last minute OR do I start right away?
_____

You've Got To Start Somewhere

"Don't let life discourage you; everyone who got where he is had to begin where he was."

-Richard L. Evans

You've Got To Start Somewhere

Discuss the meaning of this saying:

"A journey of a million miles begins with a single step."

Where were you? Where are you now?

Where do you hope to be in the future?

I hope to grow up to become an manga artist, but until then, I will work on drawing and story format. I used to work with the computer to draw better, now I practice with my friends.

Draw a map of your life based on your answers.

I was (_____), now I am (_____).

Complete five of these sentences about yourself.

I was _a baby_, now I am _a 9 yr. old_.

I was _not smart_, now I am _smart_.

I was _not good at drawing_ now I am _good with drawing_.

I was _good at spelling_, now I am _bad at it_.

I was _8 yrs old_, now I am _9 yrs old_.

You've Got To Start Somewhere

Draw a cartoon that explains the meaning of the saying:

"If you don't succeed at first, try, try again."

You've Got To Start Somewhere

Choose one or more of the following:

1) Write about how you know when to give up and how you know when to go on.

_____

_____

_____

2) Write about about a time you felt discouraged.

_____

_____

_____

Class Project:
Decide as a group a goal you would like to reach in the next week. Make a list of things that need to be done to accomplish this goal. Plan checkpoints for the week. Finish and evaluate:

How cooperative were you?
How effective were you?
How similar is the final product to what you expected?
How did you deal with people who didn't do their share?

The Golden Rule

"If the man destroys the eye of another man, they shall destroy his eye."
–Code of Hammurabi

The Golden Rule

Class Discussion:

1) Is the Code of Hammurabi fair?

2) Is revenge fair?

3) Is justice fair?

Who was Hammurabi?

_____
_____
_____
_____

Research and choose a way to present what you have learned (e.g. chart, poster, comic book, etc.).

Draw a cartoon that shows the problems with getting revenge.

The Golden Rule

Choose one or more of the following:

1) Write about a time you were treated unfairly.

_____
_____
_____
_____

2) Write about a time you treated someone else unfairly.

_____
_____
_____
_____

3) Write about what you do when you are treated unfairly.

_____
_____
_____
_____

The Golden Rule

Make up your own dictionary entry for "getting even".

_____
_____
_____
_____
_____

Write one sentence that tells what you "get" when you get even.

_____
_____
_____

How would you solve the problems of crime and punishment in this country?

Survey some people to find out what they think.

_____
_____
_____
_____
_____

Go To The Head Of The Class

"To teach is also to learn."
–Japanese proverb

Go To The Head Of The Class

Class discussion:

1) If a teacher teaches the class and no one learns, has he or she taught?   Maybe

2) The purpose of a teacher is to enable students to get along **without** a teacher.

Write one or two paragraphs about someone who taught you but wasn't a teacher.

My ~~Mom~~ Mom has taught me with math when I struggled with it. She also explained the things I did wrong on a test so I could do better. My Mom was ~~always~~ always there when I needed her.

Go To The Head Of The Class

Make a list of at least five things you need to know before you teach.

1) _____
_____

2) _____
_____

3) _____
_____

4) _____
_____

5) _____
_____

Research how someone becomes a teacher.

What does he or she have to do?
_____
_____
_____
_____

Go To The Head Of The Class

Choose one or more of the following:

1) Write about some of the most important things you've learned.

_____
_____
_____
_____
_____

2) Write about what the following things have to do with learning:

listening

_____
_____
_____

attitude

_____
_____
_____

intelligence

_____
_____
_____

Free Play

"Half our life is spent trying to find something to do with the time we have rushed through life trying to save."

-Will Rogers

Free Play

Class discussion:

1) Is time "free"?

2) Is it possible to make up lost time?

3) How does more time become too much time?

4) Can you save time?

Write a poem with the title

"Time and Time Again"

_____
_____
_____
_____
_____
_____
_____
_____

Free Play

Choose one or more of the following:

1) Write about whether you work better with too much time OR too little time.

_____
_____
_____
_____
_____

2) Write about a time that time got the best of you.

_____
_____
_____
_____
_____

3) Write about how you waste time.

_____
_____
_____
_____
_____

Free Play

Do NOTHING for five minutes. What was it like?
_____
_____
_____
_____
_____

Give a survey. Ask people: What do you do when you have nothing to do?

Publish the results.
_____
_____
_____
_____
_____

Draw a cartoon that illustrates the expression "killing time".

Remember What?

"We do not remember days, we remember moments."

- Author Unknown

Remember What?

Class discussion:

1) No day is over if you have a memory of it.

2) Why is memory selective?

Choose one or more of the following:

1) Pretend that you can have someone else's memories for a day. Whose memories do you want and why?

_____
_____
_____
_____
_____

2) There's a line from a song that says: "If I could put time in a bottle..." If you could preserve one memory from this last year, what would it be and why? Describe the memory.

_____
_____
_____
_____
_____

Remember What?

Make a chart that gives at least five suggestions for HOW to remember something (e.g.: a phone number, material for a test, directions, etc.).

Design a stamp OR a coin that commemorates a moment that is important to you.

Bring in two or three souvenirs from places, people, or events in your life.

Write how each one brings back a memory.

_____
_____
_____
_____
_____
_____

Remember What?

Draw a cartoon that shows where memories go.

Choose three or more of these memories and share them through "art".

A place you remember

A sound you remember

A taste you remember

A smell you remember

A texture you remember

A feeling you remember

A person you remember

A mood you remember

A Leave Of Absence

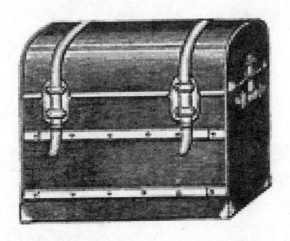

"To leave is to die a little...one leaves behind a little of oneself at any hour, any place."
—Edmond Haracourt

A Leave Of Absence

Discuss how this statement applies to the quote on the previous page:

"The minute you are born, you start to die."

If you could pack away three things (not people or pets) that belong to you in a trunk for 100 years, what would they be and why?

1) _____

_____

_____

_____

2) _____

_____

_____

_____

3) _____

_____

_____

_____

A Leave Of Absence

Choose one or more of the following:

1) Write about how it FEELS to say goodbye?

___
___
___

2) What are some things that people have left behind for you?

___
___
___

3) Write about whether or not memories can substitute for "the real thing"?

___
___
___

Imagine that today you are leaving your school and neighborhood forever. Predict what people will remember about you a year from now.

___
___
___
___

A Leave Of Absence

Make a poster that shows different ways to say "goodbye".

```
┌─────────────────────────────────┐
│                                 │
│                                 │
│                                 │
│                                 │
│                                 │
│                                 │
│                                 │
│                                 │
└─────────────────────────────────┘
```

Write a letter to someone you haven't seen in a while. Mail it.

Draw a map of your house that illustrates how someone would know you have been there.

People Are Strange

"A stranger is a friend you haven't met."

–Author Unknown

People Are Strange

Class discussion:

1) How can you feel lonely in a crowded room?

2) What is the importance of first impressions?

Write at least one paragraph as if YOU were the new kid in school.

What do you imagine it would be like? What would you do and say? What would other kids do and say? How would things look to you?

_____

_____

_____

_____

Draw what you think YOUR first impression looks like.

People Are Strange

Practice 10 different ways to say "HELLO."

1) _____
2) _____
3) _____
4) _____
5) _____
6) _____
7) _____
8) _____
9) _____
10) _____

Write a recipe for "friendship". Include ingredients and instructions.

_____
_____
_____
_____
_____

People Are Strange

Write advice, "Dear Abby" style, about how to meet people.

_____
_____
_____
_____

Choose one or more of the following:

1) Write about how a stranger can turn into a friend and how a friend can turn into a stranger.

_____
_____
_____

2) Write about a first impression you had that was wrong.

_____
_____
_____

3) Write about how you decide whether or not you want to meet someone.

_____
_____
_____

The Word Is

"Every definition is dangerous."

—Erasmus

The Word Is

Class discussion:

1) "There's always time to add a word but never to withdraw one."

2) Words do not mean anything themselves—the only meanings they have are the meanings people give to them.

Choose one or more of the following:

1) Write about a time no words were right.

_____
_____
_____
_____
_____
_____

2) Write about a time you were at a loss for words.

_____
_____
_____
_____
_____
_____

The Word Is

Make your own dictionary for the following words by writing your OWN definitions:

beautiful: To look or see something ~~silly~~ that is glamorus or cute

funny: ~~To make jokes or be~~ hilarious, silly

tall: long

wealthy: ~~Lots of~~ Lots of money

family: Group of relatives

America: ~~Country~~ Country in ~~&~~ North America

Compare your definitions to those in a dictionary. How are they alike and how are they different? Which do you think are better? Why?

The Word Is

Write a poem that has no words.

_____
_____
_____
_____
_____
_____

Using magazines, etc. make a collage with some of your favorite words (or pick a theme and find words that fit).

Do research to find out about the history of the dictionary. Also find out how words are added to the dictionary.

Talking To Yourself

"*Conscience is the inner voice that warns us someone may be looking.*"

–H.L. Mencken

Talking To Yourself

Class discussion:

How does a person "get" a conscience?

How does a conscience "work"?

How does this quote apply to the one on the previous page?
"Maturity is when you are good and nobody is around to see it."

_____
_____
_____
_____
_____
_____

Write yourself a letter congratulating yourself on a good decision you made.

_____
_____
_____
_____
_____
_____

Talking To Yourself

Think about the situations listed below, then choose one or more and list possible solutions. Next, write what your conscience tells you to do.

1) You haven't studied for an important test.
_____
_____

2) Someone you don't like wants to borrow a pencil.
_____
_____

3) A sales clerk gives you too much change.
_____
_____

4) You break something you borrowed from a friend.
_____
_____

5) You find a wallet on the street.
_____
_____

6) You want to go to the movies but don't have enough money to pay full price—however, you look young.
_____
_____

Talking To Yourself

Draw a picture of your conscience.

Choose one or more of the following:

1) Write about a time you didn't (or did) listen to your conscience.
_____
_____
_____

2) Write about three people you wouldn't want looking when you make a mistake. Explain your choices.
_____
_____
_____

3) Write about how you decide what is right and what is wrong.
_____
_____
_____

Home Sweet Home

"Home is not where you live, but where they understand you."

-Author Unknown

Home Sweet Home

Design your ideal room. Show the windows, doors, etc.
Do NOT put any furniture in it. Instead, fill the room with people and ideas that make it a place where you are understood.

Choose one or more of the following:

1) Write about a place you don't want to live.
A aporement because people make too much noise.

2) Write about who understands you.
Macaela. Macaela is really kind and she is ~~attwa~~ always there for me.

3) Write about how you feel when you are not understood.
I get mad and it annoys me.

Home Sweet Home

Make a list of all the things "home" is.
_____
_____
_____
_____
_____
_____

Who would you invite as a guest speaker to your school to talk about who you are? (In other words, who "gets you"?)
Explain your choice.
_____
_____
_____

Write the speech the person in the above activity might give about you.
_____
_____
_____
_____
_____
_____

Home Sweet Home

Make a list of five things that people would NOT be surprised to find out about you.

1) I like Burger King
2) I hate homework
3) I love to draw
4) I like music
5) I like to be funny

...and a list of five things that people WOULD be surprised to find out about you.

1) I like Horrid Henry
2) I have about 365 shopkins
3) I like creepypasta
4) I kinda like school
5) I hate Fortnite

What do you understand about your house and the people who live in it? Make a cartoon, comic book, map, or drawing that answers the question.

Come Into My Laboratory

"Discovery consists of seeing what everybody else has seen and thinking what nobody has thought."

-Author Unknown

Come Into My Laboratory

Class discussion:

1) What is the importance of doing something that has never been done before?

2) How do people get ideas?

3) Complete these sentences:
   If only there were...
   Someone ought to invent.....

In a group discuss the following :

1) How to get rid of pollution.

2) How to weigh an elephant.

3) How to make a completely fire-proof building.

4) How to make shoes so people can walk on water.

Draw a cartoon (or series of cartoons) that shows "Great Moments in Inventing History".

Come Into My Laboratory

Invent new uses for:

ping pong balls = golf ball

shoelaces = a "key holder"

can openers = carve wax

umbrellas = imaginary boat

scotch tape = use for ~~robot~~ art

gloves = puppets!

Choose three or more. Make a chart that shows your ideas.

Come Into My Laboratory

Choose one or more of the following:

1) Write about a good idea you had.

_____
_____
_____
_____

2) Write about something you wish would be discovered and/or invented.

_____
_____
_____
_____

3) Write about something you wish would NEVER have been discovered and/or invented.

_____
_____
_____
_____

The In Crowd

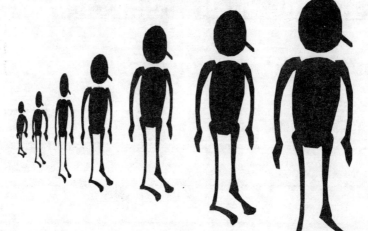

"One man with courage makes a majority."

—Andrew Jackson

The In Crowd

Class discussion:

Is courage physical OR mental? Why?

Does the majority rule?

Make up a dictionary definition for:

"A majority of one." _____

_____

_____

Write a WANT AD for a courageous person. What qualifications do people need for bravery?

_____

_____

_____

_____

_____

_____

_____

The In Crowd

Choose one or more of the following:

1) Write about a time you didn't follow the crowd.
_____
_____
_____

2) Write about how peer pressure affects what you do and say.
_____
_____
_____

3) Write about whether it is more important to you to be popular OR to be right.
_____
_____
_____

Who would you invite to the class to talk about courage? Explain your choice.

_____
_____
_____
_____

The In Crowd

Write and illustrate a fable for young children about the importance of standing up for what you believe.

Design an award for your own personal Hall of Fame. Fill out the award for three people of your choice. Explain your "nominations".

It Could Be Better!

"People ask you for criticism, but they only want praise."

–W. Somerset Maugham

It Could Be Better

Class discussion:

You are the only person you have to please. Do you agree?

It's easy to be a critic? Why or why not?

Using primarily color and line, illustrate how praise makes you feel.

It Could Be Better

Choose one or more of the following:

1) Write about a criticism that hurt.

One time ~~she~~ [my teacher] criticized me in front of the whole class. because I ~~had go~~ was crushing my test.

2) Write about what you learned from criticism.

Critisizm dosn't truly hurt you, it helps you in the future. it is t not or f not, just t

3) Write about why people are their own worst critics.

You can always do better but you don't realize it.

How does this quote apply to the above quotation?
"You can catch more flies with honey than with vinegar."

Don't be rude ~~about~~ [in] criticism. Just give positive suggestions.

It Could Be Better

Imagine that you are a critic for your local newspaper. Choose between restaurant critic, movie critic, or TV critic. After you decide, write your newspaper column and review a restaurant, movie or TV program.

Everyone loves the Teen Titans. They are funny and superheros, but can they make it better? Maybe the Titans can work on their plot. This show always mixes up the plot, so say one episode is about crime fighting, but then another one would probably be about something else!

Find five to ten less painful ways to say, "That's awful." List them.

1) You can do better...
2) You should try a little harder...
3) Maybe you can change this...
4) Try adding a little more inspration...
5) Try again with the...
6) _____
7) _____
8) _____
9) _____
10) _____

Revolving Questions

"Just when I thought I knew all of the answers, they changed all of the questions."

—Author Unknown

Revolving Questions

Create a list of five things you now know.

1) _____
2) _____
3) _____
4) _____
5) _____

What evidence do you have that people are lifelong learners?

_____
_____
_____

Write a letter to an infant giving him or her advice on how to "make it" in this world.

_____
_____
_____
_____
_____
_____
_____

Revolving Questions

"See" yourself: making a phone call, crossing the street, caring for a plant, spending money, baking a cake, or washing dishes.
What do you need to know in order to do these things? Pick three or more and make a diagram for each that shows what to do.

Choose one or more of the following:
1) Write about something you wish you had known earlier.
_____
_____

2) Write about how you know what you don't know.
_____
_____

3) Write about what is worth knowing.
_____
_____

Make a list of at least five questions for which you would like to have answers.

1) _____

2) _____

3) _____

4) _____

5) _____

Revolving Questions

Draw a cartoon that tries to explain why the questions keep changing and who (or what) changes them.

Choose one or more of the following:

1) Write about something you wish you had done earlier.
_____
_____

2) Write about how you know what to do each morning.
_____
_____

3) Write about what is worth doing.
_____
_____

In Favor Of Kids

"Children are our most valuable resource."

–Herbert Hoover

In Favor Of Kids

Class discussion:

In what ways are children the future?

How does a child make the transition into adulthood?

Write a poem or song that shares your "vision".

_____
_____
_____
_____
_____
_____
_____
_____

Write about one of your best memories.

_____
_____
_____
_____
_____
_____

In Favor Of Kids

Choose one or more of the following:

1) Write about the little child still left in you.

_____
_____
_____

2) Write about how you want to contribute to the world when you are older.

_____
_____
_____

Make up a dictionary definition for the word "potential". Design a symbol that shows the meaning of the word.

_____
_____
_____
_____

Take a survey of your classmates to find out what they want to contribute to the world. Make a graph to share the results.

In Favor Of Kids

Choose THREE things you do NOT want to be when you grow up. Give at least two reasons for each choice.

_____
_____
_____
_____
_____
_____
_____

What kind of world would you like to see for you, your children, your grandchildren, etc.?

_____
_____
_____
_____
_____
_____

There is a popular advertising slogan that says: "Be all that you can be." What will you be? How will you get there? Write a plan.

Your Two Faces

> "Everyone is a moon and has a dark side which he never shows anybody."
>
> –Mark Twain

Your Two Faces

Class discussion:

"Live so that when you die, the mourners will outnumber the cheering section."
— *Source Unknown*

Write a poem with the title:

"The Me Nobody Knows"

_____
_____
_____
_____
_____

Write yourself a letter about what you think might happen if people found out about your "other" side.

_____
_____
_____
_____
_____

Your Two Faces

Make a list of at least five things people like about you.

1) _____
2) _____
3) _____
4) _____
5) _____

Make a list of at least five things you like about yourself.

1) _____
2) _____
3) _____
4) _____
5) _____

Make a graph to show how much of you is hidden away.

Your Two Faces

Choose one or more of the following:

1) Write about where you go when you want to be alone.

_____
_____
_____
_____

2) Write about a little known fact about you that might surprise someone.

_____
_____
_____
_____

Think of yourself as having two lives—public (outer) and private (inner). Write about how your two lives blend together to make YOU.

_____
_____
_____
_____
_____

Inside And Out

"What really matters is what happens in us, not to us."

-Author Unknown

Inside And Out

Write a prescription for healing your inner self.

When I feel mad or sad, I usally take a nap or I draw.

Write a poem or make a collage about the "happenings" in your life.

Inside And Out

Get a paper bag. On the outside, write words that tell what has happened to you in your life. On the inside (on slips of paper), write words that tell your feelings about your life.

Outside growth is usually seen in inches and pounds. Inside growth is harder to see. Design a special instrument for measuring inside growth.

Include directions for how it works.

_____
_____
_____
_____
_____
_____
_____

Inside And Out

Choose one or more of the following:

1) Write about one of the most significant events in your life (good or bad).

_____
_____
_____
_____

2) "Five percent of life is what happens to us. Ninety-five percent is how we react to it." (Source Unknown) Explain.

_____
_____
_____
_____

3) Write about how this quote applies to your life?

"Some people wish for something to happen while other people make it happen."
                     — Michael Jordan
_____
_____

Chasing Rainbows

"We all live under the same sky, but we don't all have the same horizon."

–Konrad Adenauer

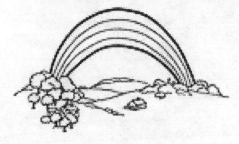

Chasing Rainbows

Class discussion:
Some people think that when you set goals, you should be realistic, others say to be idealistic. If you are realistic, you won't be disappointed. If you are idealistic, you'll go further than you thought. What do you think?

Draw a picture of your horizon line.

Make a list of at least four goals you have.

1) _____
2) _____
3) _____
4) _____

Write one sentence about how this list is your horizon.

_____
_____

Chasing Rainbows

Write a letter to yourself that you will open in one year. Write about where you hope to be, what you want to be doing, things you want to have accomplished, etc. Put your letter in a safe place and open it in a year.

_____
_____
_____
_____
_____
_____
_____
_____
_____
_____

Make a travelogue of where you think you will need to "travel" before you reach your biggest goal.

_____
_____
_____
_____
_____
_____
_____

Chasing Rainbows

Interview at least five people about their goals. Make a chart or graph of the different goals.

Write one sentence about what you learned from doing this.

Seeing Red!

"People who fly into a rage always make a bad landing."

—*Will Rogers*

Seeing Red!

Class discussion:

1) When you lose control, what else do you lose?

2) What does anger get for you?

Draw a picture of your temper.

Brainstorm and make a chart (or list) of at least five things to do INSTEAD of losing your temper.

1) _____
2) _____
3) _____
4) _____
5) _____

Seeing Red!

Choose one or more of the following:

1) Write about ways you show that you are angry.
_____
_____
_____
_____

2) Write about a situation in which you lost control.
_____
_____
_____
_____

Write a nursery rhyme for children which will teach them to control their temper.

_____
_____
_____
_____
_____

Seeing Red!

In "David Letterman style", what are the top 10 reasons to "keep your cool"?

1) _____
2) _____
3) _____
4) _____
5) _____
6) _____
7) _____
8) _____
9) _____
10) _____

Make an "anger collage".
Include: angry colors, weather, places, things in nature, foods, people, ideas, and appropriate words.

I Gotta Be Me

"Accept me as I am—only then will we discover each other."

—Federico Fellini

I Gotta Be Me

Class discussion:

Is it possible to change another person?

Write a poem with the title:

"I've Got To Be Me!"

_____
_____
_____
_____
_____
_____
_____
_____

Make up a dictionary definition for ACCEPTANCE.

~~Acceptance~~ Acceptance means when your accepted into or onto something.

I Gotta Be Me

Draw a non-physical self-portrait. Draw an outline of you. Fill it in with the feelings, experiences, likes, dislikes, that make you, you.

Make a timeline of a friendship. Include all major landmarks and events.

Make a souvenir for the class that captures the essence of you. Just like the Statue of Liberty "says" New York City, what "says" you? Include an explanation.

I Gotta Be Me

Choose one or more of the following:

1) Write about a time you were accepted.
I was once accepted to be my friend's friend

2) Write about a time you accepted someone else.
I once (had) to accept Peyton.

3) Write about something that was hard for you to accept.
Peyton playing with us so I don't get my butt suspended

Make a map that shows how to discover people.

Believe It Or Not!

"Nil credam et omnia cavebo." (Believe nothing and be on guard against everything.)

—Latin proverb

Believe It Or Not!

Class discussion:

People believe what they want to believe. Do you agree?

Draw the difference between UNBELIEVABLE and NOT believable.

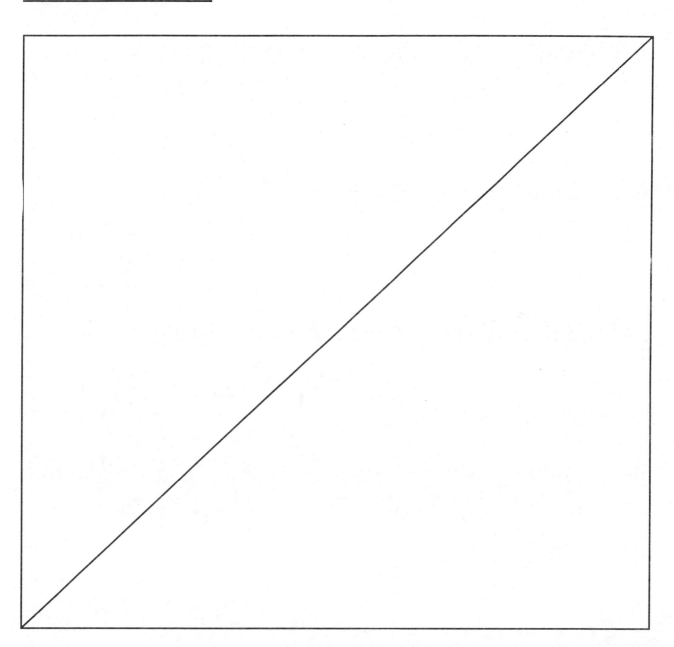

Believe It Or Not!

Choose one or more of the following:

1) Write about the risks you take when you trust someone.
_____
_____

2) Write about who you trust and why you trust them.
_____
_____

3) Write about a time you were fooled.
_____
_____

4) Write about how you know when to trust someone.
_____
_____

Make some warning signs (in the style of traffic signs) to show people when they should be cautious.

Believe It Or Not!

Trust Scale: For each of the following, assign a number from 1-10. 1 = DON'T TRUST AT ALL. 10 = TRUST COMPLETELY.

__7__ Setting your alarm clock.

__4__ Asking a stranger for directions.

__5__ Telling a friend a secret.

__8__ Getting your friend's opinion about a movie.

__8__ The grades on your report card.

__7__ Baking cookies from a recipe in a magazine.

__9__ Going to the police with a tip about a crime.

__10__ When your parent tells you, "It is for your own good."

Write about a time someone disappointed you.

Once I was promissed to be brought to wherever I wanted, but, I was later brought to the mall. My mom only bought clothes and she knows I hate going ~~to~~ to the stores and buying clothes.

The Grass Is Always Greener

"He that has one eye is a prince among those that have none."

—Thomas Fuller

The Grass Is Always Greener

Class discussion:

How is "wanting what you get" different from "getting what you want"?

Make a list of at least five items for each of the following topics:

"Things I envy about other people"
1) They are better at a subject
2) They have phones / better or more items
3) They have more friends / popularity
4) Pets
5) Looks

"Things other people might envy about me"
1) I am good at drawing
2) Smart
3) Amazing Friends
4) Family
5) Life

When you finish, write a one sentence observation about your lists.

People ~~have~~ may have things or traits that I want, but ~~other people~~ might want the same thing

The Grass Is Always Greener

Write a story about how the saying "green with envy" got started.

_____
_____
_____
_____
_____
_____

Draw or write to explain the differences between:

admiration and envy

_____
_____
_____

hope and envy

_____
_____
_____

ambition and envy

_____
_____
_____

The Grass Is Always Greener

Choose one or more of the following:

1) Write about some things you want that you don't already have.
___

2) Write about where people get ideas to want things.
I think when you see or hear something, ~~your~~ the part of the brain that is in charge of your intrest tells your brain that you want it.

3) Write about when enough is enough.
___

Draw a picture or cartoon to illustrate the following saying: "The one who dies with the most toys, wins!" While you are drawing, think about the message.

- 103 -

Playing With Blocks

"People are lonely because they build walls instead of bridges."

-Author Unknown

-104-

Playing With Blocks

Words are the bridges we build to reach each other. Make a list of some of those words.

_____
_____
_____
_____
_____
_____

What are some clues that tell you a person is lonely?

_____
_____
_____
_____
_____

Write an advice column with questions and answers.
Topic: Loneliness.

_____
_____
_____
_____
_____

Playing With Blocks

In "David Letterman style", what are the Top 10 Reasons for "Reaching Out to Someone"?

1) _____
2) _____
3) _____
4) _____
5) _____
6) _____
7) _____
8) _____
9) _____
10) _____

Construct a bridge of your own design.

```
┌─────────────────────────────────────────┐
│                                         │
│                                         │
│                                         │
│                                         │
│                                         │
└─────────────────────────────────────────┘
```

What do you need to know to make it work?

_____
_____
_____

Playing With Blocks

Choose one or more of the following:

1) Write about a time you were lonely.

_____
_____
_____
_____

2) Write about the differences between being ALONE and BEING LONELY.

_____
_____
_____
_____

Draw the outline of a brick wall. On each brick, write a word that keeps people out or keeps you in.

Take A Picture

"It is difficult to see the picture when you are inside the frame."

—*R.S. Trapp*

Take A Picture

Class discussion:

1) What are some ways to remove yourself from a situation or experience?

2) When is it necessary for a person to step out of his or her frame?

3) What do people mean when they say you are too close to a situation?

What is your "frame of reference"? Draw a picture of it.

In a letter to yourself, explain which is harder for you: looking out OR looking in?

_____
_____
_____
_____
_____
_____

Take A Picture

Facts ↗

List three topics about which you are objective.

1) _____

2) _____

3) _____

→ opinion or biased

List three topics about which you are subjective.

1) _____

2) _____

3) _____

When people say, "I'm really into this," they mean:

_____

_____

_____

Illustrate the difference between being OBJECTIVE about something and being SUBJECTIVE about something.

Take A Picture

Choose one or more of the following:

1) Write about some things in which you are VERY involved.

_____
_____
_____

2) Write about a time you put yourself in someone else's shoes.

_____
_____
_____

Think of every situation as having "BIG ROCKS" and "little rocks". The "BIG ROCKS" are the big picture, the "little rocks" are the details. If SCHOOL is the topic, what are the "BIG ROCKS" and what are the "little rocks"? Draw the outlines of boulders and pebbles and fill in with your answers.

- 111 -

You Don't Say

"What a good thing the first man had—when he said a good thing, he knew nobody had said it before!"

—Mark Twain

You Don't Say

Class discussion:

Discuss the differences between quantity and quality of speech.

Why have proverbs been passed down from generation to generation?

Make up a dictionary definition for ORIGINALITY.

~~the ability~~ It means that something is creative/unique (my handwriting)

Write the word "originality" in an original way.

Originality   Originality
              Originality

On a blank piece of paper, make your own "graffiti wall".

You Don't Say

Write four original proverbs. Choose from the following topics:

money   friends   school   love
children   happiness   competition   disappointment

1. _____

2. _____

3. _____

4. _____

Draw your favorite on a poster.

You Don't Say

Choose one or more of the following:

1) Write about something you wish you would have said.
_____
_____

2) Write about the meaning of a popular proverb.
_____
_____

3) If it is true that "you are what you say", write about what that makes you.
_____
_____

Research three of the following people:

Toulouse Lautrec	Winston Churchill	Dizzy Gillespie
Lou Gehrig	Americus Vespucci	Charles Dickens
Napoleon	Maria Tallchief	Wyatt Earp

From what you now know about these people, write something memorable you think they could have said. Write it in the form of a quotation.

1. _____
2. _____
3. _____

An Important Message

"It is more important to be human than it is to be important."

—Author Unknown

An Important Message

Class discussion:

Are all people important?

What is it about humans that make them important?

Write a dictionary definition for the phrase: "Keeping it in perspective".

_____
_____
_____
_____

Design a commemorative stamp or coin for someone you consider to be important.

An Important Message

Create a poster OR a bumper sticker with your message describing what you feel is an important thing to remember about being important.

[   ]

Illustrate the meaning of the saying: "He is too big for his britches" OR "Don't let it go to your head."

[   ]

On TV they say: "We interrupt this program to bring you this important message." What important message do you have for the world?

_____
_____
_____
_____

An Important Message

Choose one or more of the following:

1) Write about the most "human" person you know.
_____
_____
_____
_____

2) Write about the most important person you know.
_____
_____
_____
_____

3) Write about a time you felt important.
_____
_____
_____
_____

Letting Go

"Don't push the river, it flows by itself."

—F. Perls

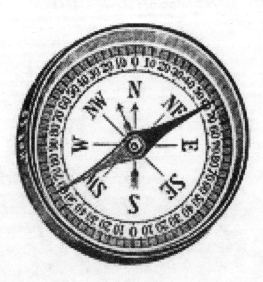

Letting Go

Class discussion:

It is easier to swim with the current than against it.

How are "giving up" and "leaving it to fate" the same and different?

Choose one or more of the following:

1) Write about a time you were impatient.

_____
_____
_____
_____

2) Write about a time things were out of your control.

_____
_____
_____
_____

Letting Go

<u>Draw a picture of "FATE."</u>

<u>Write a poem called</u>

"If My Mother Had Wings, She'd Be An Airplane!"

_____
_____
_____
_____
_____
_____

<u>Who is freer in society? The person who follows all the rules so completely that he or she doesn't even have to think about them OR the person who rebels against the rules? Choose one side. Imagine you are on the debating team. Write your argument.</u>

_____
_____
_____
_____
_____
_____

Letting Go

Who or what makes things happen? Write at least one sentence for each of the following:

1) A sled going downhill

_____
_____
_____
_____

2) Grades on a report card

_____
_____
_____
_____

3) High ratings for a TV show

_____
_____
_____
_____

4) Losing a football game

_____
_____
_____
_____

Turning Red

"Man is the only animal that blushes. Or needs to."

—Mark Twain

Turning Red

Class discussion:

Is embarrassment self-created OR other-created?

Write and illustrate a fable: "What Embarrassed The Caveman!"

Turning Red

Draw what embarrassment looks like. Explain your artwork.

Create a cartoon about embarrassment.

"This too will pass!" How does this statement apply to the above quotation?

_____
_____
_____
_____

Turning Red

Choose one or more of the following:

1) Write about a time you were embarrassed.
_____
_____
_____
_____

2) Write about things that make you self-conscious.
_____
_____
_____
_____

3) Write about how you handle embarrassment.
_____
_____
_____
_____

Write an apology to someone for embarrassing him or her.
_____
_____
_____

Do You See What I See?

"People only see what they are prepared to see."

—Emerson

Do You See What I See?

Class discussion:

When someone says, "I see" what does he or she mean?

What are things that influence what you see?

Can two people ever see EXACTLY alike?

Choose one or more of the following:

1) Write about something you thought you saw but didn't.

_____

_____

_____

2) Write about the difference between "looking" and "seeing".

_____

_____

_____

Draw a cartoon with the caption: "Now you see it, now you don't!"

Do You See What I See?

A lot of "seeing" depends on close observation. Choose three or more of the following to observe and write about:

1) One strand of your hair
_____
_____

2) A fingernail
_____
_____

3) A line made by a pencil
_____
_____

4) The ceiling of your classroom
_____
_____

5) The differences between your right and left hands
_____
_____

Do You See What I See?

Answer these questions using your visual memory:

1) Does the front door of your school swing in or out?
_____
_____

2) How many closets are in your house?
_____
_____

3) On a sink, which side is the hot water on?
_____
_____

4) What color are your teacher's eyes?
_____
_____

5) Whose picture is on the nickel?
_____
_____

How did you do? Write one sentence that tells about the experience of doing this.
_____
_____

Sharpen Your Pencil!

"Life is the art of drawing without an eraser."

—John Christian

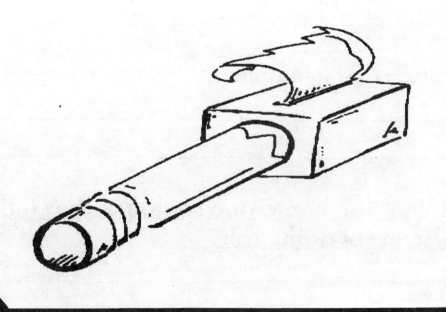

Sharpen Your Pencil!

Class discussion:

How can mistakes work for you?

Why erasers don't really work!

"Those who do not make mistakes do not make anything."

"Stupidity is doing the same thing over and over again and expecting a different result." (Source Unknown) Illustrate this quotation.

Sharpen Your Pencil!

Make a chart that shows how to avoid making mistakes.

```
┌─────────────────────────────────────────────┐
│                                             │
│                                             │
│                                             │
│                                             │
│                                             │
└─────────────────────────────────────────────┘
```

Get a piece of drawing paper and a pencil and draw three things or people in your classroom. DO NOT use your eraser—even once!!! DO NOT get another piece of paper or start over, even if you make a mistake. When you finish, describe how this experience made you feel and what you learned by doing it.

_____

_____

_____

_____

Invent a game of chance. Play it with several others. Write about the experience.

_____

_____

_____

_____

Sharpen Your Pencil!

Choose one or more of the following:

1) Write about a mistake that worked for you.
_____
_____
_____
_____

2) Write about a mistake you keep making.
_____
_____
_____
_____

3) Write about a chance you took.
_____
_____
_____
_____

Did You Ever Have To Make Up Your Mind?

"When you have to make a choice and you don't make it, that in itself is a choice."

-William James

Did You Ever Have To Make Up Your Mind?

Choose one or more of the following:

1) Explain this quote, "Choosing is existence (life). If you don't choose, you don't exist".

_____
_____
_____
_____

2) Which is worse: making a poor decision OR not making a decision at all?

_____
_____
_____
_____

"The cruelest lies are often told in silence." (Source Unknown) How does this quote apply to the above quotation?

_____
_____
_____
_____

Did You Ever Have To Make Up Your Mind?

Choose one or more of the following:

1) Write about a time you changed your mind.
___
___
___
___

2) Write about a decision you found easy to make.
___
___
___
___

3) Write about a decision you found difficult to make.
___
___
___
___

Did You Ever Have To Make Up Your Mind?

MAKE A DECISION: Write your answers. (Choose one or more.)

1) It is up to you to choose the first U.S. citizen to travel to Mars. You may pick anyone you want (aside from yourself), famous or non-famous. This is an extremely great honor for the person you pick and the whole country is waiting to hear your decision. Who will it be? Explain your decision.

_____
_____
_____
_____

2) You have just been given $30 to spend any way you want. You really need school supplies but you desperately want to go to the movies with your friends and buy a CD. There is no other way you can get the money for any of these things. What will you spend the money on? Explain your decision.

_____
_____
_____
_____

Beginnings And Endings

"Fear not that your life shall come to an end, but rather fear that it shall never have a beginning."

-Author Unknown

Beginnings And Endings

Class discussion:

There are no beginnings or endings—there is just now.

"A journey begins with a single step." - Source Unknown

Design a symbol for LIFE. Explain your design.

Find a way to prove that you are alive. (You cannot say your heart is beating!!!)

_____
_____
_____
_____
_____

Beginnings And Endings

What are you just now beginning? Make a list.

_____
_____
_____
_____

What things are coming to an end? Make another list.

_____
_____
_____
_____

Compare the lists and write a sentence about what you learned.

_____
_____

Someone opens up YOUR biography: "The Life and Times of _____." What is written on the first page? What is written in the middle? What is written on the last page?

_____
_____
_____
_____

Beginnings And Endings

Choose one or more of the following:

1) Write about things that are scary and not scary about being alive.

_____
_____
_____

2) Write about how you make your life count.

_____
_____
_____

Draw a picture to show how life is a continuum (circle).

Draw yourself on the cover of Newsweek or Time magazine. What is the story about? Write the first paragraph.

_____
_____
_____

Other Titles Available from N.L. Associates, Inc.

Nathan Levy's Stories with Holes (Volumes 1-20)
by Nathan Levy
Each book in this 20 volume series contains stories for children ages 7-77. These books are great fun as a classroom activity or for playing a game with your child. They stimulate children's critical and creative thinking skills as they try to "fill in the holes" in each of these stories.

Not Just Schoolwork Volume 1
by Nathan Levy & Amy Burke
This book combines superb activities for critical thinking, written expression, and creativity. It is a wonderful tool to motivate teachers and students. The units are open-ended and can be used from grades 3-12. The activities in this book bring child-centered integration of learning to life for teachers and pupils.

Write, From the Beginning (*Revised Edition*)
by Nathan Levy and Amy Burke
Children in grades K-5 have a lot to say about themselves and their world. The writing materials in this book break away from the same old assignments and forms. This book keeps children highly interested and improves writing skills.

Thinking and Writing Activities for the Brain Book 1

Whose Clues Volumes 1-6

Intriguing Questions Volumes 1-6

There are Those

Nathan Levy's Test Booklet

Please write or call to receive our current catalog.
N.L. Associates, Inc., P.O. Box 1199, Hightstown, NJ 08520
(732) 656 - 7822
www.storieswithholes.com

Dynamic Speakers
Creative Workshops
Relevant Topics

Nathan Levy, author of the <u>Stories with Holes</u> series and <u>There Are Those</u>, and other nationally known authors and speakers, can help your school or organization achieve positive results with children. We can work with you to provide a complete in-service package or have one of our presenters lead one of several informative and entertaining workshops.

- Practical Activities for Teaching Gifted Children
- Critical Thinking Skills
- Teaching Gifted Children in the Regular Classroom
- How to Read, Write and Think Better
- Using <u>Stories with Holes</u> and Other Thinking Activities
- Powerful Strategies to Help Your Students With Special Needs be More Successful Learners
- The Principal as an Educational Leader

and many more

Nathan Levy, author and consultant

Nathan Levy is the author of more than 40 books which have sold almost 250,000 copies to teachers and parents in the US, Europe, Asia, South America, Australia and Africa. His unique <u>Stories with Holes</u> series continues to be proclaimed the most popular activity used in gifted, special education and regular classrooms by hundreds of educators. An extremely popular, dynamic speaker on thinking, writing and differentiation, Nathan is in high demand as a workshop leader in school and business settings. As a former school principal, company president, parent of four daughters and management trainer, Nathan's ability to transfer knowledge and strategies to audiences through humorous, thought provoking stories assures that participants leave with a plethora of new ways to approach their future endeavors.

Please write or call to receive workshop information.

N.L. Associates, Inc., P.O. Box 1199, Hightstown, NJ 08520
(732) 656 - 7822
www.storieswithholes.com